A Child's History of TEXAS

**Text and Drawings By
Sarah Jackson
And Mary Ann Patterson**

EAKIN PRESS

Dedicated to the
Young Readers of Texas

Published in the United States of America
By Eakin Press, P.O. Drawer 90159, Austin, TX 78709-0159

ISBN 0-89015-056-7

TEJAS

"Tejas!" meant "friends" and was the greeting used by early Indian tribes in our state. Later the word became "Texas" and was taken as the name for our state.

Six flags have flown over Texas:

SPAIN   FRANCE   MEXICO

TEXAS   CONFEDERACY   UNITED STATES

The mockingbird is the state bird, the bluebonnet is the state flower, and the pecan is the state tree. Our state song is "Texas Our Texas" and our motto is "friendship."

EARLY INDIANS IN TEXAS

For hundreds of years, Indians were the only people living in Texas. They lived outdoors hunting, fishing and gathering plants. The early Indians talked with sign language and painted pictographs .or "word pictures" on cave walls, rocks or hide.

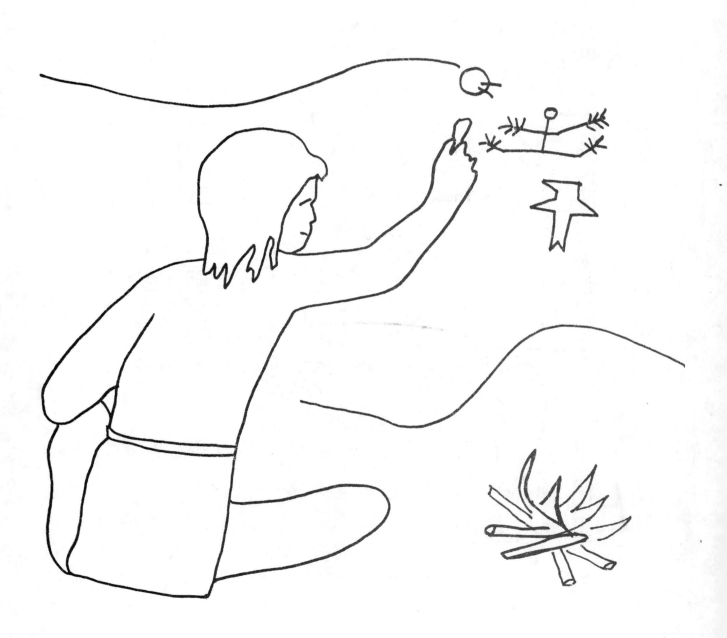

THE INDIANS OF EAST TEXAS

The Caddo and Wichitas Indians of East Texas lived in huts made of grass instead of teepees. Their huts were shaped like bee-hives. These two tribes were chiefly a farming people who remained in a particular place. Corn was one of their best crops. They made clay pots and jugs for cooking and drinking. These Indians were believed to be the most advanced Indians living in Texas.

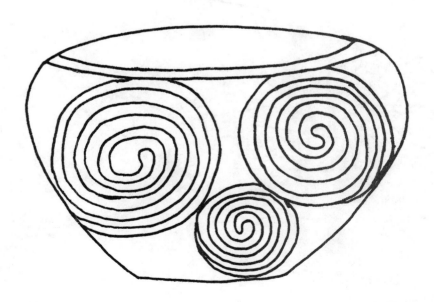

INDIANS OF EAST TEXAS

THE INDIANS OF WEST TEXAS WERE HUNTERS

The Comanches, Kiowas, and the Lipan Apaches were fierce warriors and hunters. The Comanches painted their faces red. Buffalo was the main object of the hunt. The Indians ate the meat and used the skin and fur for clothing. The West Texas Indians lived in teepees which could be taken down easily and carried from place to place.

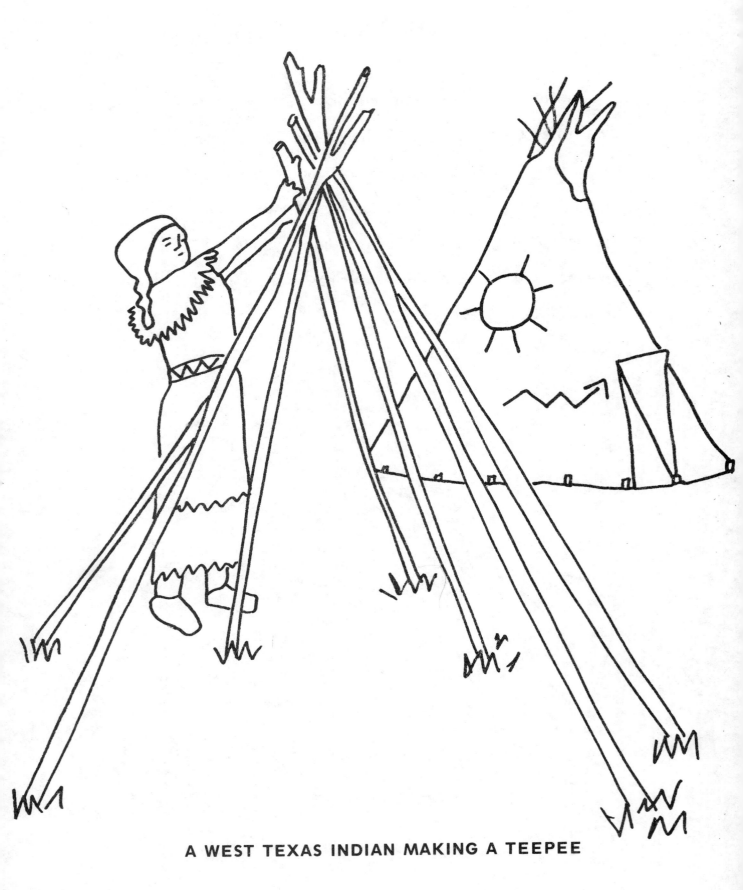

A WEST TEXAS INDIAN MAKING A TEEPEE

INDIAN TEXAS

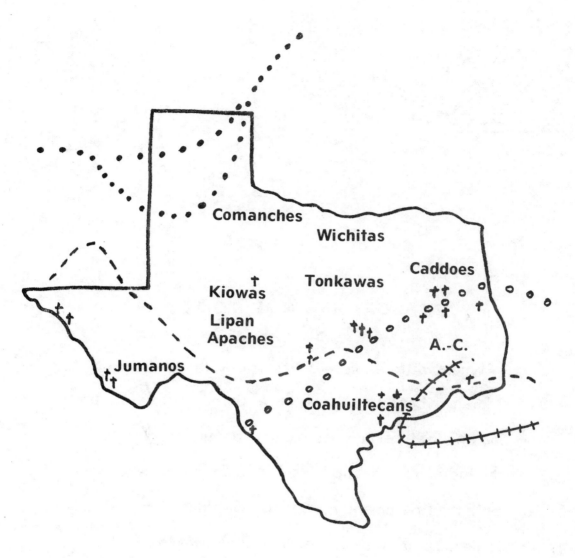

Comanches

Wichitas

Caddoes

Kiowas

Tonkawas

Lipan
Apaches

A.-C.

Jumanos

Coahuiltecans

– – – Cabeza de Vaca 1535-36

• • • • Coronado 1540-42

++++++ La Salle 1685-86

o o o o o Saint Denis 1713

✝ Early Missions

A.C. = Alabama-Coushatta Indians

EXPLORERS CAME TO TEXAS

When white explorers first came to Texas many Indian tribes were living here. Some explorers were looking for treasure, some came to teach religion to the Indians and set up missions, and some were traders. Both the French and the Spanish wanted to send settlers to Texas and claim this large territory for themselves.

CABEZA DE VACA

The first Spanish explorer to visit Texas came as a result of a shipwreck. In 1528 Cabeza de Vaca and his men ran into rough seas off the Texas coast. The Spaniards became prisoners of the Indians. Cabeza de Vaca and three others from the expedition, one a Moor, escaped and traveled across Texas to safety in Mexico. These men gave the first reports to Europe describing what Texas was really like. The buffalo was among the unusual facts he reported. He also reported that he found no gold but that the Indians had said there was much gold and large cities in Texas.

CORONADO CLAIMS TEXAS FOR SPAIN

The Spaniard, Coronado, whose gold-plated armor shone bright in the sun, headed an expedition of 250 armored horsemen and 70 foot soldiers. They were looking for the fabulous land of "Quivira," the land of gold and silver. The search for gold led the Spaniards across the plains of Texas. They left disappointed, finding no treasures.

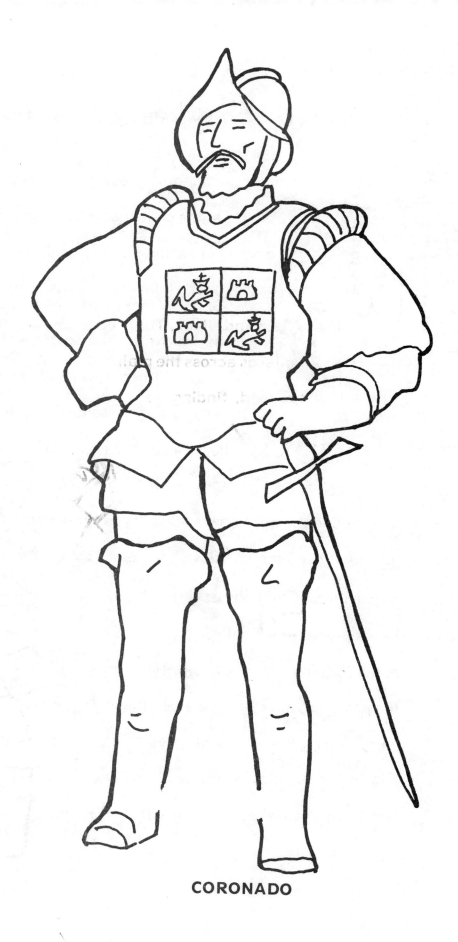

CORONADO

EARLY MISSIONS IN TEXAS

San Francisco de los Tejas

was the first Spanish mission in East

Texas. Father Massanet consecrated

the little log mission in 1690.

The mission was far

from settled areas. Supplies were

scarce and the mission was destroyed three years later.

But the first Spanish mission in East Texas was very

important. It helped establish the claim of Spain to

the region. Nevertheless, by 1700 East Texas belonged

to the Indians almost as completely as at any time in

the past. The only Europeans living in Texas at the time

were the few Spaniards who lived in the missions along the

Rio Grande. Today a replica of San Francisco de los Tejas

can be visited about 25 miles from Crockett.

MISSION SAN FRANCISCO DE LOS TEJAS, 1690

THE FRENCH CLAIM TEXAS

The first European settlements in Texas were made in the late 17th century by the Spanish along the Rio Grande. The French had claimed Louisiana as their own, naming the area for King Louis XIV of France. La Salle, an explorer for the French government, took 400 Frenchmen and sailed from the mouth of the Mississippi River into the Gulf of Mexico to reach Texas. In 1685 La Salle landed on the Texas coast at Matagorda Bay. He established the first French colony in Texas, Fort St. Louis. After much misfortune the fort was destroyed by an Indian raid in 1689. La Salle's effort was important, however, because it gave the French a vague claim to Texas and it revived Spanish interest in East Texas.

LA SALLE CLAIMS TEXAS FOR FRANCE

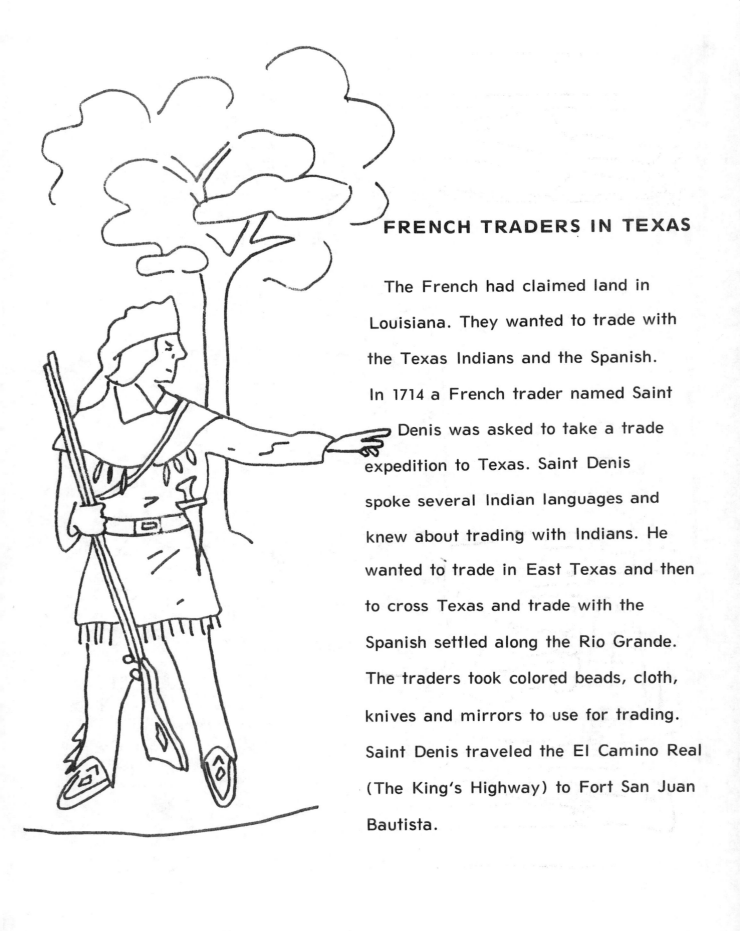

FRENCH TRADERS IN TEXAS

The French had claimed land in Louisiana. They wanted to trade with the Texas Indians and the Spanish. In 1714 a French trader named Saint Denis was asked to take a trade expedition to Texas. Saint Denis spoke several Indian languages and knew about trading with Indians. He wanted to trade in East Texas and then to cross Texas and trade with the Spanish settled along the Rio Grande. The traders took colored beads, cloth, knives and mirrors to use for trading. Saint Denis traveled the El Camino Real (The King's Highway) to Fort San Juan Bautista.

THE FOUNDING OF SAN ANTONIO

The need for a halfway stop between the Spanish settlements on the Rio Grande and those in East Texas became necessary. Therefore, the Spanish established a new settlement in 1718 on the San Antonio River. Mission San Antonio de Valero (The Alamo) was established. This was the beginning of the town of San Antonio. After a few years it became the capital and largest town of Spanish Texas.

THE RESETTLING OF EAST TEXAS

By the end of the French and Indian War (1763) the French had lost their claim to Louisiana. The Spanish owned the land west of the Mississippi River and the English now owned the land east of the river. Since the French were no longer a threat, the Spanish felt it was unnecessary to have missions or settlements in East Texas. They moved about 500 settlers to San Antonio.

The East Texans did not like living in San Antonio and in 1779 Gil Y'Barbo led many of them back home, settling in Nacogdoches. Nacogdoches became one of the most important towns in Spanish Texas. The stone house which Gil Y'Barbo built is one of the oldest buildings in Texas. Texas' first newspaper, "Graceta de Tejas" was printed here in 1813.

The Old Stone Fort can be visited today on the Stephen F. Austin State University campus in Nacogdoches.

THE OLD STONE FORT IN NACOGDOCHES

JEAN LAFITTE

The French pirate, Jean Lafitte, made Galveston Island his headquarters in 1817. Known as "The Pirate of the Gulf," Lafitte had nearly 1000 men working for him. The pirates would attack and rob the Spanish ships in the Gulf of Mexico. About four years later Lafitte and his men were run out of Texas by a U.S. warship.

MOSES AUSTIN ASKS TO BRING AMERICANS TO TEXAS

Some enterprising Americans wanted to settle Texas
in hope of making their fortunes. In 1820 Moses Austin
went to San Antonio and asked the Spanish governor for
permission to settle a colony of Americans in Texas.
With the help of Baron de Bastrop the petition was
granted, but Austin died before the grant was filled.

STEPHEN FULLER AUSTIN

Moses Austin's dying wish was for his son to carry out the plans for a colony in Texas. Stephen Fuller Austin completed the contract with the Mexican government and served Texas so well that he is known as "The Father of Texas." With the permission of the Mexican government Austin offered large tracts of land at small cost to Americans who would settle in Texas. Each family who settled would receive approximately 4,605 acres of land. He made it clear that he would accept only persons of good character. Because of Austin's hard work the way was opened for Americans to enter Texas and by 1831 almost 6000 people lived in the colonies he had established.

MRS. JANE LONG

Mrs. Jane Long was one of the most courageous characters from early Texas history. Her husband, who had led an expedition to Texas, built a small fort at Bolivar Point on Galveston Island. Mrs. Long, her small child, and a black servant girl remained on the abandoned island to await Dr. Long's return from Mexico. The two women endured a long and difficult wait. They fired their only cannon to frighten away Indians who came too near. They dug oysters from the beach to keep from starving. Finally, two years later (1822), word came of Dr. Long's death in Mexico. Mrs. Long lived many more years and was one of the first 300 settlers who received land from Stephen F. Austin.

HOW THE PIONEERS CAME TO TEXAS

Many early settlers came to Texas in
covered wagons. The wagons were pulled by oxen or
horses. There were no stores so they carried their
water, food and clothes with them. The big wagons
moved slowly with cows and horses following behind.
Hundreds of families left their old homes and traveled
through Texas on El Camino Real—The King's Highway.
These men, women and children were pioneers. They were
brave to come to a new part of the country where
they did not know what they would find.

HOW THE PIONEERS CAME TO TEXAS

HOW THE EARLY SETTLERS LIVED

Early settlers in Texas built their homes out of logs they had made from trees. They had to grow their own food and make their own clothes. Children were taught the "3 R's"—reading, writing, and arithmetic—at home by their mothers.

HAVING SCHOOL IN A FRONTIER HOME

LIFE ON THE RANGE

Cowboys spent many days on the range driving herds of cattle to market. All the cattle were branded with their owner's special brand. The trails were dusty and long for the cowboys, but it brought great wealth to the owners.

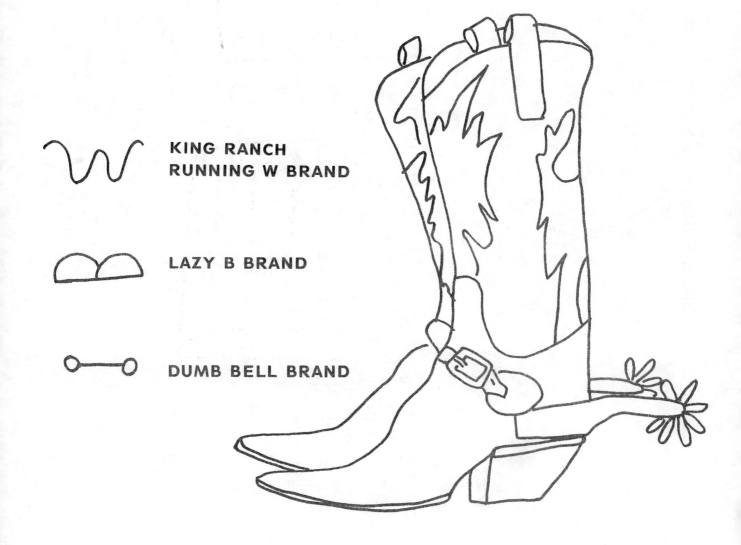

**KING RANCH
RUNNING W BRAND**

LAZY B BRAND

DUMB BELL BRAND

CHUCK WAGON ON THE RANGE

SAN FELIPE DE AUSTIN

Stephen F. Austin made his home in San Felipe de Austin. It became the capitol of his colony. His house was the typical dog-trot cabin like many colonists built. Austin was elected President of the convention of 1832 at San Felipe when the Texans asked that Texas be made a separate Mexican state.

THE TEXAS RANGERS

The Texas Rangers were organized in 1835. Their job was to range the frontier to warn the settlers of Indian raids. Rangers were also used to bring law and order in places where cowboys were rowdy. They fought badmen who were stagecoach robbers, horsethieves, or cattle rustlers. Since 1935 the Texas Rangers have been associated with the Highway Patrol.

A TEXAS RANGER

"VICTORY OR DEATH!"
THE BATTLE OF THE ALAMO

Santa Anna, the leader of the Mexican
Army, hoped to crush the Texans who were trying
to form a republic of their own. The Texans
were unprepared when Santa Anna's army reached
San Antonio on February 23, 1836.

Col. William B. Travis was commander
over all troops in San Antonio. Travis' 160
men were greatly outnumbered by the several thousand Mexican
soldiers. The Texans occupied the Alamo as their fort.
Davie Crockett and Jim Bowie, the maker of the famous
Bowie Knife, were among those at the Alamo. James Bonham
was sent with a message to bring aid to Travis and his men.
Bravely, he returned alone, a white scarf tied to his hat
as proof that he was a friend and not a foe.

On March 6, Santa Anna began his massive attack. The first attackers were put off, but the Mexican numbers were too great and soon they were scaling the walls of the Alamo. The seige lasted about an hour. No Texan fighting man survived the battle.

The men who fought with Travis at the Alamo must be recognized as among the most heroic in Texas history. The defeat of the Alamo gave the Texans their battle cry: "Remember the Alamo!"

BONHAM RETURNS BY NIGHT TO THE ALAMO

A TEXAS PATRIOT FIGHTS FOR FREEDOM

EARLY DEFEAT

The Texans met one defeat after another.

Many were killed at Goliad.

Many Texans fled to the United States.

General Sam Houston wondered how to keep his army.

He retreated to the eastern part of the state.

As he moved eastward many men joined Houston's army.

JAMES W. FANNIN COMMANDED THE TROOPS AT GOLIAD.
THEY WERE CAPTURED AND EXECUTED SOON AFTER THE
FALL OF THE ALAMO.

THE CONSTITUTION

The Texans needed a Constitution to give them unity.
A Constitutional Convention was formed February 1, 1836,
and quickly finished its work. The Chairman, and
writer of the Constitution, was George C. Childress.
Others on the Committee were James Gaines, Edward Conrad,
Collin McKinney and Bailey Hardeman. Sam Houston was
re-elected Commander-in-Chief. David Burnet became temporary
President of the Republic. Thomas J. Rusk was Secretary
of War.

DECLARATION OF INDEPENDENCE WAS SIGNED MARCH 2, 1836

THE RUNAWAY SCRAPE

March 2, the Declaration of Independence was signed at Washington-on-the-Brazos. Pres. Burnet and his Cabinet had to flee immediately. They became known as the Government On Horseback. The settlers also fled before the Mexican Army. This became known as the Runaway Scrape.

PRESIDENT BURNET AND HIS CABINET DESERTED WASHINGTON-ON-THE-BRAZOS.

VICTORY AT SAN JACINTO

Sam Houston is known to all Texans as the "Hero of San Jacinto." The Texas forces had retreated after earlier defeats. Santa Anna's Army followed and finally the two armies met. On April 21, 1836, Houston led the Texans in a surprise attack. The Texans ran on the enemy camp shouting, "Remember the Alamo! Remember Goliad!" This famous battle which won Texas her freedom lasted only 20 minutes. Sam Houston was wounded in the knee, Santa Anna was captured and Texas had won her battle for independence!

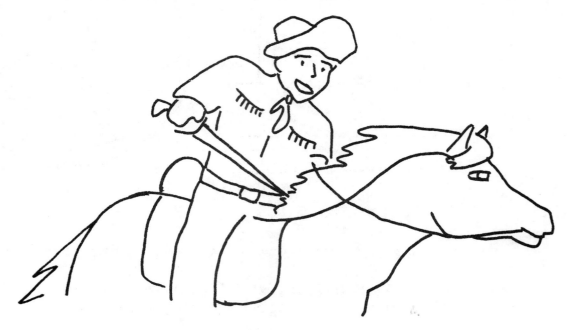

SAN JACINTO MONUMENT   HOUSTON, TEXAS

THE WAR ENDS

The Treaties of Velasco ended the war.
The boundry between Mexico and Texas was the Rio
Grande River.

   There was an election after the fighting ended.
Sam Houston, "Hero of San Jacinto," was chosen
President of the Republic and Mirabeau B. Lamar,
Commander of the Texas Cavalry at San Jacinto, was chosen
Vice-President. Stephen F. Austin, Thomas Rusk
and Henry Smith made up the Cabinet. Oct. 3, 1836
the new government assembled at Columbia but the
capital soon moved to Houston. It was in Oct. 1839
that the government was moved to Austin when Lamar
became President.

THE FIRST CAPITOL   WASHINGTON-ON-THE-BRAZOS   1836

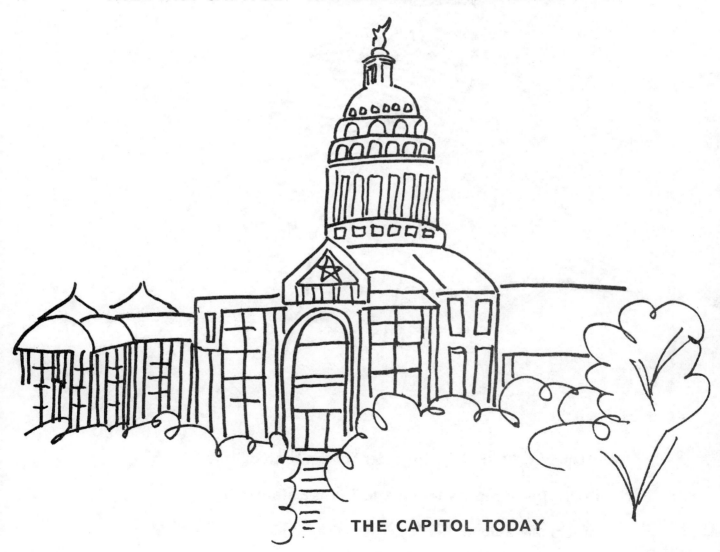

THE CAPITOL TODAY

A STATE OR A REPUBLIC?

Many Texans, among them Mirabeau B. Lamar, wanted
Texas to remain a Republic. Many more Texans, including
Sam Houston, wanted Texas to become a state of the United States.

On Dec. 29, 1845 the President of the United States,
Polk, signed the act that made Texas a state of the
American union.

GOVERNOR ANSON JONES LOWERED THE LONE STAR FLAG
FEBRUARY 19, 1846, AND TEXAS BECAME A STATE OF THE
USA.

FRONTIER FORTS

The Mexican War of 1846-48 added to the United States a vast territory comprising the present states of New Mexico, Arizona and California. The southern route to this area, through Texas, needed the protection of the western frontier fort. Fort Davis, named in honor of Secretary of War Jefferson Davis, was designed to protect the San Antonio-El Paso Road. Restored today, it affords a splendid example of the frontier post.

Listen to the sounds of a dress parade of 1874 on the empty field.

FORT DAVIS NATIONAL HISTORIC SITE.

OUTSTANDING EXAMPLE OF SOUTHWESTERN FRONTIER FORT.

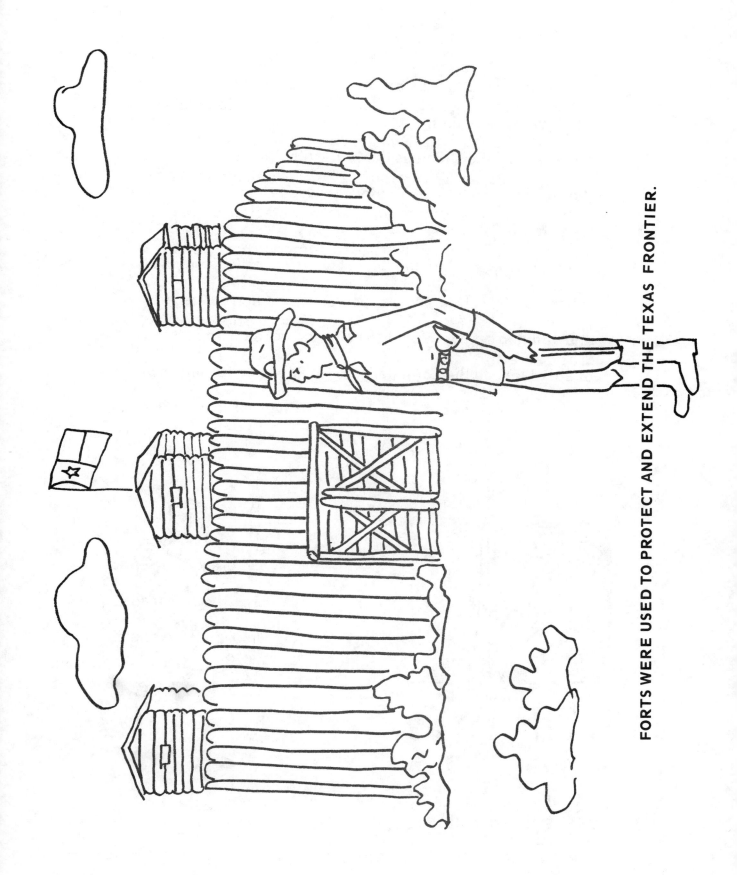

FORTS WERE USED TO PROTECT AND EXTEND THE TEXAS FRONTIER.

THE CIVIL WAR

As war clouds gathered over the nation, Texas' heritage and kinship lay with the South. Texas joined the Union as the 28th state. When she withdrew to join the Confederacy, she was the 7th state to do so.

Governor Sam Houston did not want Texas to leave the Union. On March 16, 1861, a special convention convened and voted to secede. Because he would not sign an oath of allegiance to the Confederacy, Houston had to step down as Governor. Edward Clark became Governor in his place.

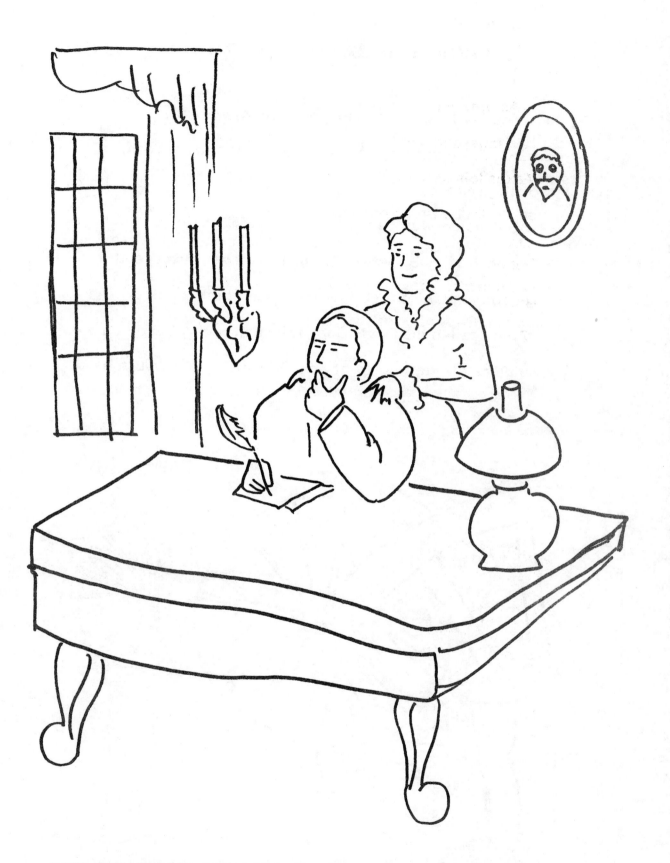

SAM HOUSTON'S MOMENT OF DECISION. MARCH 16, 1861

CIVIL WAR BATTLES IN TEXAS

The Civil War battles fought in Texas were the result of Union efforts to blockade trade and gain control of the seaports.

Galveston was captured in Oct. 1862. Efforts under General John B. Magruder in November succeeded in recapturing the city. Under the leadership of Dick Dowling, 47 men called the Davis Guards turned back 5,000 Union soldiers attempting to attack Beaumont and Houston.

CIVIL WAR CANNON

BATTLE OF SABINE PASS. DOWLING'S MEN HELD OFF 5,000 UNION SOLDIERS.

TEXAS—A LEADER IN INDUSTRY

After the surrender of the South in 1865, Texas again found her place as a state in the United States. There was a period of struggle known as Reconstruction. But the state moved steadily towar the economic gains and prosperity that makes Texas a leader in the nation. Much of the regained strength was based on the railroad.

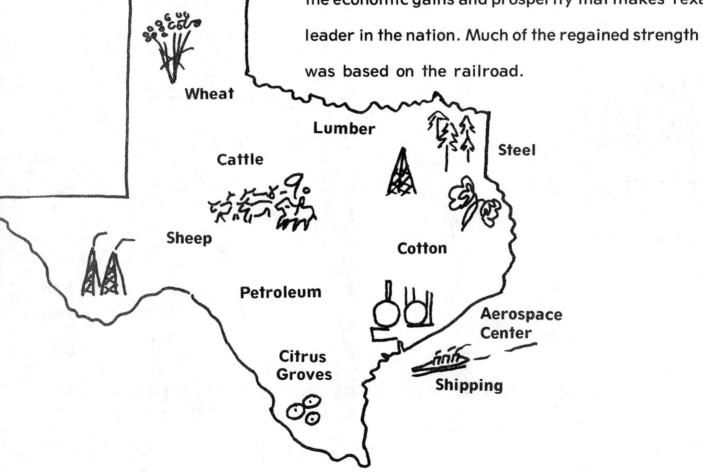

Wheat

Lumber

Cattle

Steel

Sheep

Cotton

Petroleum

Aerospace
Center

Citrus
Groves

Shipping

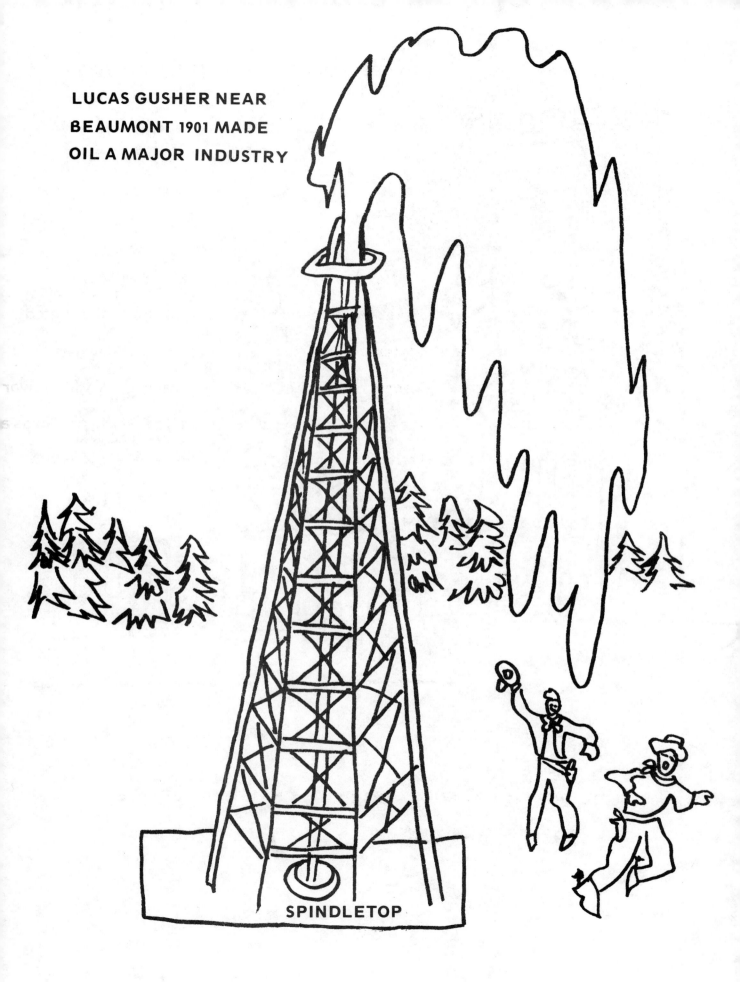

LUCAS GUSHER NEAR
BEAUMONT 1901 MADE
OIL A MAJOR INDUSTRY

SPINDLETOP

OIL DERRICKS DECORATED WITH CHRISTMAS LIGHTS

KILGORE, TEXAS

ANOTHER SOURCE OF POWER . . . . . ON THE TEXAS PLAINS

EDUCATION IS BIG BUSINESS.

THE LARGEST UNIVERSITY IN THE SOUTH IS THE UNIVERSITY OF TEXAS FOUNDED IN 1883.

THE LONGHORN COW, A FAMOUS TEXAN
TODAY BEEF AND DAIRY CATTLE ARE IMPORTANT TO THE
STATE'S ECONOMY.

LUMBER WAS A LEADING INDUSTRY IN THE EARLY REPUBLIC AND ALSO IS TODAY.

CITRUS IN SOUTH TEXAS

TEXAS LEADS THE NATION IN SHRIMPING

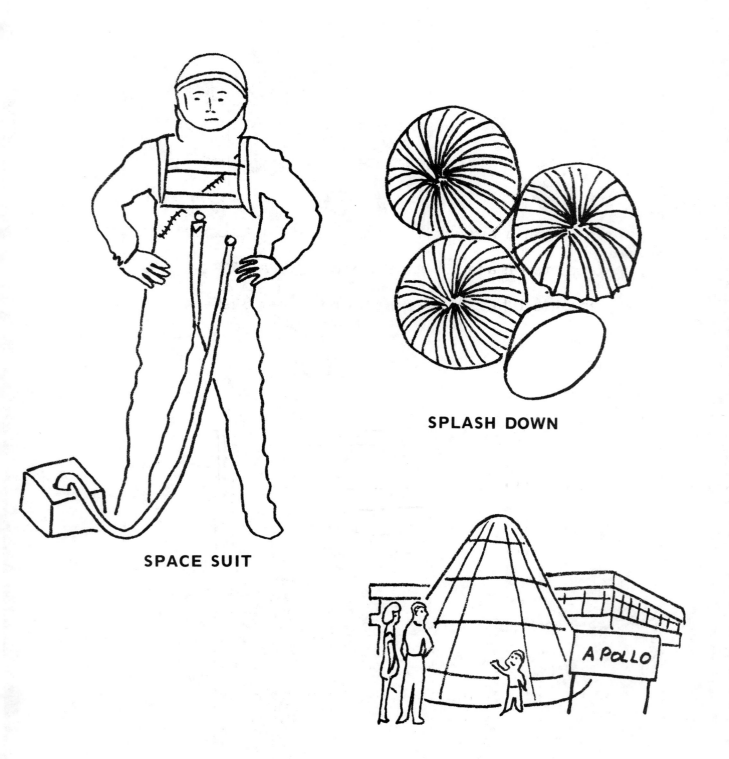

SPACE SUIT

SPLASH DOWN

APOLLO

THE SPACE CENTER IN HOUSTON IS AN INDUSTRY IN ITSELF.

WORLD WAR I

Almost 200,000 Texans served in the armed forces during the war. Thousands of troops were trained in Texas, for the dry, warm climate provided good training conditions. Dozens of military camps were established throughout the state, and the favorable climate was a factor in the location in Texas of most facilities for training the newly established Air Force.

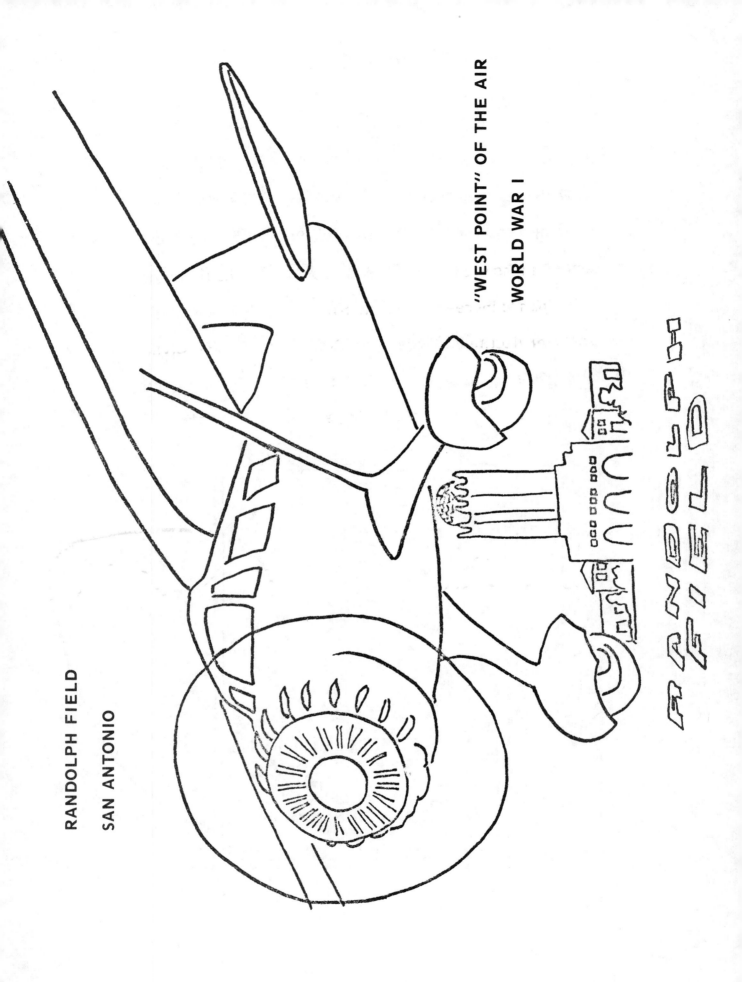

RANDOLPH FIELD

SAN ANTONIO

"WEST POINT" OF THE AIR

WORLD WAR I

RANDOLPH FIELD

WORLD WAR II

Just as in the First World War, Texans flocked
to the armed services. More than 750,000 served.
Again, hundreds of thousands of soldiers, sailors
and airmen were trained at Texas bases and camps.
Texans in every walk of life worked long hours at their
jobs to increase production and then they helped in
servicemen's clubs, Red Cross activities, or Civil
Defense projects in their "spare" time. At home and
abroad, Texans did their part in the struggle.

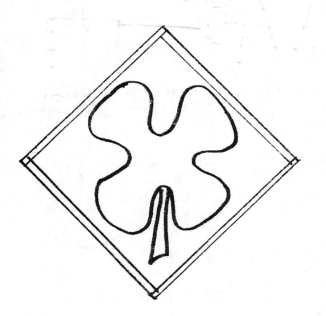

USS TEXAS WAS AT IWO JIMA IN WORLD WAR II

THE SHIP IS NOW AT SAN JACINTO BATTLEGROUND

NATIONAL LEADERSHIP

TEXAS IS ASSOCIATED WITH THREE PRESIDENTS OF THE USA

DWIGHT D. EISENHOWER WAS BORN IN DENISON, TEXAS

JOHN F. KENNEDY WAS ASSASINATED IN DALLAS IN NOV. 22, 1963.

LYNDON BAINES JOHNSON WAS THE FIRST TEXAN TO BE
PRESIDENT OF THE UNITED STATES.

LBJ LIBRARY IN AUSTIN, TEXAS

RECREATIONAL PARADISE

TEXAS IS A STATE OF CONTRAST

SEASIDE OR CITY

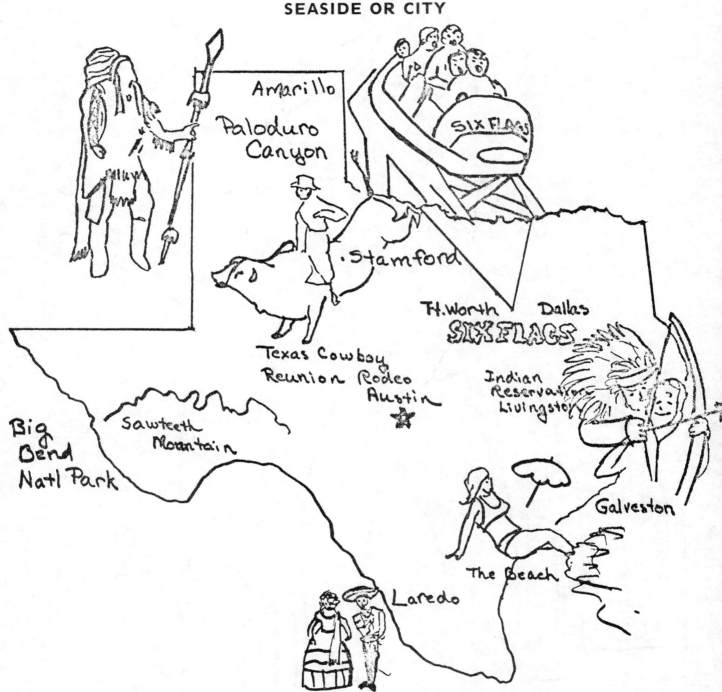

STARK DESERT OR MILE-HIGH MOUNTAINS

THICK WOODLAND AND EXPANSIVE LAKES

BIG TEX
OF STATE FAIR OF TEXAS FAME   DALLAS

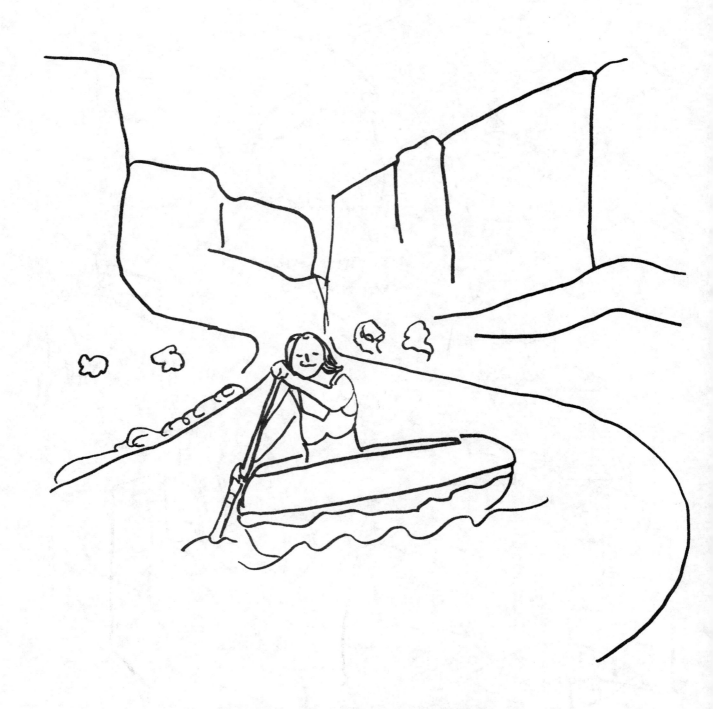

PADDLING DOWN THE RIO GRANDE

BIG BEND NATIONAL PARK

AUTUMN FESTIVALS

AUTUMN TRAILS
WINNSBORO

EAST TEXAS
YAMBOREE

GILMER

TYLER ROSE FESTIVAL

PAUL GREEN'S OUTDOOR DRAMA "TEXAS"

THE HEMISFAIR IN SAN ANTONIO

THE ASTRODOME
HOUSTON

BASEBALL, ONE EXCITING EVENT UNDER THE DOME.

AT THE BEACH

TEXAS GULF COAST